IT'S A DOGGONE

Shame

CURIOUS CANINE CRIMES & CATASTROPHES

SHELLY SCHULTHESS BARSON

PLAIN SIGHT PUBLISHING
AN IMPRINT OF CEDAR FORT, INC.
SPRINGVILLE, UTAH

ISBN 13: 978-1-4621-1527-3

Published by Plain Sight Publishing, an imprint of
Cedar Fort, Inc.
2373 W. 700 S., Springville, UT, 84663
Distributed by Cedar Fort, Inc., www.cedarfort.com

Cover and page design by Angela D. Baxter
Cover design © 2014 by Lyle Mortimer
Edited by Daniel Friend

Printed in the United States of America

10 9 8 7 6 5 4 3 2 1

Printed on acid-free paper

TO OUR DOG, JAI.

CONTENTS

ANIMAL NOSES

WE DON'T HAVE stuffed animals with noses. Not one.

They're not allowed.

The first nose to go belonged to a delightful little Build-A-Bear fellow that our daughter, Maddy, brought home from her eighth birthday party. She had lovingly filled him with white fluff, ceremoniously tucked his little red silk heart inside his soft chest, dressed him in a pink t-shirt, and named him Bamboo.

Bamboo was Maddy's favorite stuffed friend. He could often be seen dangling from her hand or occupying a most favored position amid the pillows on her bed. He was her little buddy.

Yet Bamboo was not alone in Maddy's heart—or her home. Across the gulf of Maddy's room, a mind that was to the bear's mind as ours are to those of the beasts that perish, an intellect vast and cool and unsympathetic, regarded Bamboo's nose with envious eyes, and slowly and surely drew his plans against it. And in the early morning hours came the great disillusionment.

Jai, the faithful family canine, became the ender of noses.

Maddy awoke the next morning to find Bamboo noseless, demoralized, and with an expression best described as "shocked." He had lost his sense of smell.

Jai seemed to have calculated his nose-maiming with amazing subtlety and to have carried out his preparations with well-nigh perfect dexterity. Bamboo's shiny little nose was gone, but nothing else was disturbed or otherwise untoward. In fact, Jai's uncanny and meticulous nose-amputation might have gone unrecognized but for the fact that his inner nose-devouring beast could not now be sated. It seams that once you have tasted stuffed-animal nose, there's no going back. And so the carnage began.

Jai didn't stop with Bamboo, you see. Oh no, far from it. Other stuffed critters soon fell victim to Jai's insatiable shiny-black-button-nose desire. A brown bear, a blue monkey, two white bunnies, a giraffe, and a spotted cow—all noseless within a week.

Jai doesn't bother with the eyes—just the nose, as though delighting in the horrified looks he leaves in his wake.

V

VI

Of course, precautions were taken. Jai was banished from Maddy's room. Stuffed animals were placed on high, out-of-reach shelves. But in the end, Jai prevailed. There are no stuffed animal noses in our house anymore.

Jai now slumbers more peacefully.

This charming tale of woe from our canine ne'er-do-well started us sharing some of his antics online, and Dog-Shame.com was born. Now, with 75,000 Facebook Friends and countless submissions from other dog owners, the all-in-good-fun tradition continues on our website and in this book, where we laugh at our dogs' antics. In the end, we're celebrating not only their antics but also our most beloved friends. In the words of John Grogan, "It's just the most amazing thing to love a dog, isn't it? It makes our relationships with people seem as boring as a bowl of oatmeal." (With a tip of the hat to H.G. Wells)

★ The ★
DOGS

★ ★ ★ ★ ★

1

I CAN'T TELL THE DIFFERENCE BETWEEN BONES AND DOLLS SO I EAT BOTH

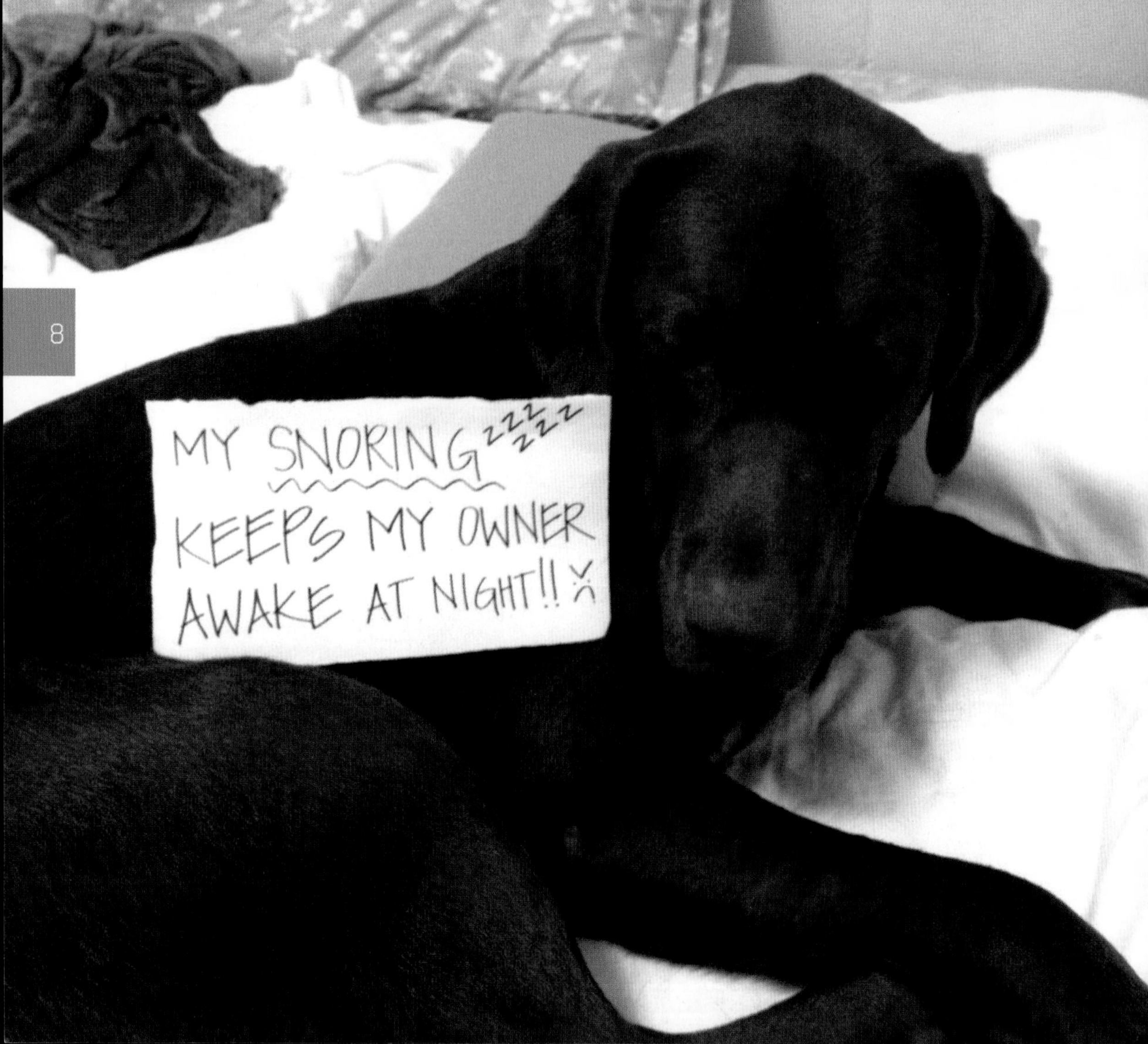
MY SNORING
KEEPS MY OWNER
AWAKE AT NIGHT!!

I ATE THE
COUCH.
MoMs Mad
AT Me.

IM A GOOD
DOG.
THEY MAKE ME
WEAR SIGNS
ANYWAY

The
FALSELY
Accused
— AWARD —

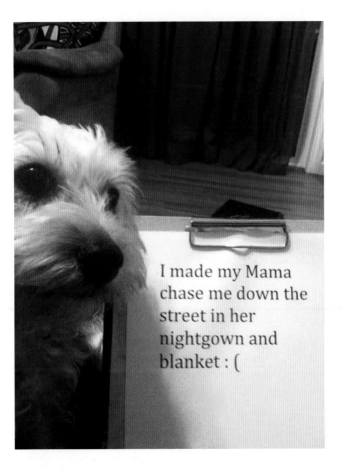

I made my Mama
chase me down the
street in her
nightgown and
blanket : (

JAI vs. THE PIZZA DELIVERY GUY

IT TAKES SOME SERIOUS GUTS to ring our doorbell in the dark.

We were having a night in with a pay-per-view show and decided to order some pizza. When the delivery guy knocked on the front door, Jai (a Bouvier) woke up and decided we were under attack. For those of you who have never pushed our doorbell, it's quite a show; a hundred-pound wrecking ball of dark hair and flashing teeth hits the front door with more force than a Mack truck, accompanied by ferocious barking and deep-chested vocals that are far more than intimidating. (The entire front of the house literally shakes.) The pizza guy was sure that a werewolf had been unleashed and that he was about to be ripped limb from limb.

Jeff commanded Jai to stop barking (which he did), but when he turned the doorknob and pulled on the door to open it, he discovered that the delivery guy wasn't so sure that was a good idea. He had a hold on the doorknob on the other side of the door and was pulling on it to keep the door shut. Jeff didn't really understand what was happening, and a few seconds of tug-of-war took place at the front door, Jeff on one side and the pizza guy, his foot on the doorframe for added leverage, on the other.

It ended well enough. We got our pizzas. The delivery guy got a 25 percent tip and made off with a little extra cash and a great deal of relief that he was still in possession of all his limbs. Jai, his duty completed, went back to sleep.

I ate the
eyeball off
Mom's sock
monkey hat.

63

9 English Muffins
I'VE DONE IT BEFORE
AND
I'LL DO IT AGAIN
Just sayin.....

The ★
REPEAT
Offender
— AWARD —
★ ★ ★ ★ ★

JAI (THE BOUVIER) VS. MECHAGODZILLA (THE PONY)

OUR WORLD INCLUDES HORSES. We have three: Keiki, Maverick, and Moon. Jai, our family Bouvier, routinely tags along with us when we go to the barn to ride inside the arena or up the surrounding mountain trails. Jai's been around horses since he was a puppy, and he's well behaved, keeping a close but respectful distance. The horses usually ignore him. He just doesn't pose much of a threat to a 1,200-pound animal wearing steel shoes.

Ponies, on the other hand, are different.

For those of you who don't know about ponies, let me drop some knowledge on you: they are not horses. Ponies are different. They're small, which means that they're often not consistently saddled or ridden, but they're too big to really train in the same way that you would train a dog. Pull on a pony's halter, or leash, and he's likely to pull back twice as hard. This lack of training and discipline means that ponies are usually the terror of the barn. They're almost universally ill-tempered ruffians.

They'll charge, bite, kick, and generally go ahead and express themselves in a number of physical ways that result in experienced stable hands keeping one eye open and on them at all times.

MechaGodzilla was a Shetland pony at the barn.

One fine summer day, we were at the barn walking out to the pasture to round up Keiki and Maverick for a trail ride. The birds sang, the bees buzzed, and all was right with the world. Jai, as usual, padded alongside, content in his world of heavenly pasture smells. Softly bounding from thicket to stream and on again, he casually raised his head and locked eyes across the pasture with someone new and interesting.

Staring back at Jai was MechaGodzilla the pony. He stood there, lock-legged, ears back, and tail weaving threats behind him—the very image of short equine scorn and disdain. The only thing separating them was a three-pole wooden fence, a short run of pasture, and the natural order of Jai's universe in which a pony does not challenge him to a duel.

Now, for those of you who know even less about Bouviers than you do about ponies, here's another knowledge bomb: they don't back down. And Jai, you see, is a Bouvier.

Jai, noting the scorn and not one to be intimidated by any lowly herbivore, wasn't going to let some squat little grass-eater with enlarged molars get the better of him. No, sir. He stopped dead in his tracks, raised every hair on his back, and emitted a low, deep, ghoulish noise that seemed to originate from below the deepest pits of Hades. To call it a mere growl would be to do it a terrible disservice. This utterance was a call to battle as feral and low as that uttered by any beast that ever stalked the dark places of the Earth. It made you believe in werewolves.

Jai, the hundred-pound horse walloper, sized up his newfound nemesis, a rotund little pot-bellied grass-pooper that had the gall to eyeball him and challenge his doghood. This could not possibly be happening.

Jai growled a second time. Time stood still.

MechaGodzilla stamped a mocking hoof . . . and then he snorted . . . and then he lifted his tail and let fall his ultimate insult.

Jai had had enough. A hundred-pound pony-walloping ball of canine fury rocketed toward MechaGodzilla. In two beats of a hummingbird's wings, Jai was at the fence. Burrowing under the bottom pole in an instant, he launched himself at his target. (Clearly the fact that MechaGodzilla outweighed him by a good four hundred pounds was no deterrent.)

Not to be outdone, MechaGodzilla the pony pinned his ears, lowered his head, and charged.

We call the moment of their first meeting "The Big Bang." There was an explosion of sorts as pony met dog, and the two transformed into a new element: a rolling ball of flashing hooves, paws, mane, tail, teeth, and dirt.

It ended well enough. After bouncing most of the way across the field, they rolled apart, called a cease-fire, and went their separate ways.

The brouhaha ended and order was restored. Jai 1, MechaGodzilla 0.

Jai still pads past the pony's pasture with a practiced nonchalance and a tongue-lolling smile as he samples the smells on his way to the horses. You probably wouldn't notice, but he walks just a little bit taller along that particular fence line.

For Jai, the universe makes sense again.

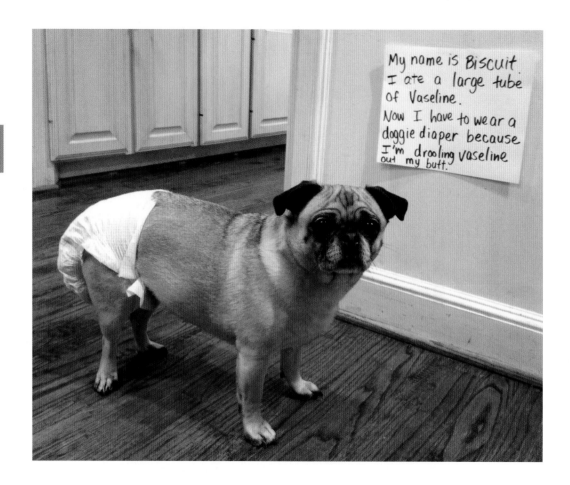

I may look big and tough, but I cry when you are gone.

The
LOVER
Not a Fighter
— AWARD —

My name is Lefty. I prune my Grandad's Plant every year right before he gets back FLORIDA. Always the Same Plant. ☺

The
BOOKWORM
Chihuahua
— AWARD —

My name is Riley and I steal tomatoes from my mom's garden even if they aren't ripe

★ The ★
Tomatoes are like
CRACK
— AWARD —
★★★★★

I AM <u>NOT</u> A SMART DOG...

Life is like a box of chocolates

My name is Mr. Tank,
I ate cockroach then
I lick mommy's face
Seems like she luv it :)

The
RAN
Afoul
AWARD

My spring
scent is
Eau de
Dead Deer

I go to the beach and eat from the fishermans bait bucket when they are not looking

The
DOG SHAME
Hall of Fame

I knocked a $600 camera onto the floor and broke it because my owner went to the bathroom.

I DON'T LIKE CHANGE!!

— Kita

I'm the new toilet paper puppy model!!!

I GO TO THE NEIGHBOURS' GARDEN TO TERRORIZE THE <u>CHICKENS</u> AND WILL DO IT AGAIN IF I CAN GET THROUGH THE BARRIER YOU PUT TO STOP ME! (x.x)

AFTER A BRIEF SABBATICAL, I'VE ONCE AGAIN RUBBED MYSELF IN POO.
(I'M POUTING AFTER MY BATH)

ABOUT THE AUTHOR

SHELLY SCHULTHESS BARSON

Born first in a litter of five, Shelly grew up amid the quaking aspens and tall pines of her grandfather's cattle ranch in Wyoming, riding horses and whispering with dogs. As a little girl she learned to love animals, and it's been said that her first true love was a shaggy giant of a black lab named O'Malley. Her favorite things are feeling the wind between a horse's ears, the word *gobsmacked*, cowboy boots, and puppy breath. She lives in Park City, Utah, with her husband, daughter, three horses, a cockatoo, and the family bouvier, Jai. She spends her time pursuing more of her favorite things (see above).